A SKEPTIC'S GUIDE TO PSYCHOLOGY

A SKEPTIC'S GUIDE TO PSYCHOLOGY

WILLIAM GLADSTONE & MARISA MORIS

INTUITION MEDIA

TABLE OF CONTENTS

PREFACE

Before starting on this book Marisa cleared the space of entities and many ascended masters and Higher Souls appeared. They discussed the differences between being connected to ascended masters and manifesting as an ascended master. Every human being is connected to an ascended master but only those who evolve beyond their lower chakras manifest the vibration of an ascended master. This is why there are human beings who do horrible things such as the 2016 murders in Orlando, Florida of 49 innocent people at the Pulse nightclub. It is by raising their vibration that individuals can connect to their Higher Souls and the ascended masters then connect to those souls. Our books are being written to help each reader learn to do this for the benefit of the entire planet and indeed the universe itself.

Among the ascended masters, spirits and souls contributing to this book are the Higher Souls of Lao Tzu, Freud, Juno and Einstein. Of course St. Germain appeared as well. When not in the energy of these sessions, I remain skeptical that these energies are real but as you will discover in the following conversation there is much information that will be useful in understanding your own ego and your opportunity to become your highest and best self. I studied psychology, anthropology and related social sciences at Yale College and Harvard University so have a particular interest in this topic.

—William Gladstone

Chapter 1
Introduction

WILLIAM: So, we're ready to start the book. The idea for today is that we should do a "Skeptic's Guide to Science." I was motivated or inspired by Freud's appearance to possibly that we should just limit it and do a "Skeptic's Guide to the Ego" or a "Skeptic's Guide to Psychology" because Freud is known—

MARISA: Shut up! I heard—I'm not even joking—I heard psychology earlier when you said science. I was walking. Right there I heard, "What about a 'Skeptic's Guide to Psychology'?"

WILLIAM: Okay. So that makes sense. Let's do a "Skeptic's Guide to Psychology."

MARISA: Oh my god, that's creepy.

WILLIAM: We're delighted to have Freud here. I have many questions for Freud. I will warn Freud right upfront that you are not going to be the only psychologist who we are going to consult on these topics. There are many, many people who have used psychology for good and bad and continue to do so, and there have been many misunderstandings about your work.

MARISA: He says, "And those pompous assholes have messed all of my shit up!"

WILLIAM: Exactly. I've had—.

MARISA: Wow. Is he known to be an ass? Not an ass but just very like—

WILLIAM: Without being politically correct, he was German at a time when Germans were somewhat overbearing. He certainly didn't suffer fools easily and was very, very confident that his realizations and insights were the most important realizations and insights of the time and that he should be considered the father of psychology.

MARISA: He says, "Well, you know…"

WILLIAM: "Well of course I am."

MARISA: He says, "Considered? It's fact."

WILLIAM: Well, there you go. I will say in, you know, deference to other great thinkers of the time including someone that Freud at first was friends with and then broke with, Carl Jung, I believe had greater insights actually than Freud in terms of concepts such as the collective unconscious—

MARISA: He says "J-U-N-G, yes, yes. That is Jung, yes, yes." Oh my god. Carl Jung is here. He's got this wavy body and he feels like he's from another planet.

WILLIAM: And he was other-worldly in his insights. He introduced concepts that went much beyond the focus that Freud had on human consciousness at the level of the individual ego and the id and the super ego. Jung went beyond those concepts in terms of how human beings are actually connected, much more accurately as we're finding out at the level of what I would call their soul groups. And Freud did not deal with these concepts at all. So, Freud I'm going to give you the floor.

MARISA: He says, "But you must understand and you, you, you will appreciate this because I've been listening, I've been listening to you. I've been listening to all of you. Yes, yes, I am here. Yes, yes, I'm a part of this channel. Yes, yes, yes. We're all part of the same soul group. Yes, yes, yes. We hear it, we hear it, we watch it, we see it. We hear all of you and yes, much of what is said just goes 'woo' right over her head, and sometimes it comes through, and sometimes all of it comes through. And it's like watching a baseball game or a game of golf and you just see us swing and a whiff—you missed the ball, and then she just laughs and says okay, and then we get it through another way. So, it is almost like watching a golf game or a baseball game when watching the three of you, Bill, Marisa, and Gayle, together because it is quite amusing. And I must just say that now—"

And his mom says, "You pompous…you like to cut people down and make them feel less than you so that you can feel better." His mom just said that.

WILLIAM: This is Freud's mom?

MARISA: Yeah. "You want to make them feel less so you can feel better." And he goes, "Shut up, mom." She's behind him.

WILLIAM: Well, now we know the true stimulation for Freud's theory. His relationship with his mother.

MARISA: The mom is in his head. The mom is right behind him. He goes, "Shut up, mom."

WILLIAM: I think it's safe to say that Freud has mom issues.

MARISA: Freud has mommy issues. She goes, "Mommy issues." She's pointing at herself. But he says, "What's quite interesting indeed, and you will appreciate this because I have heard you, you want the human to be the genius. And our friend up here doesn't want to let you think that. I think it is most important to understand the vehicle and the mechanics of the vehicle because if the vehicle isn't working, then how does the soul drive? How does the spirit drive? So, these guys over here are going to talk about the philosophy and the theology behind soul groups and all of the stuff that is inside of us and I feel that it is very important to understand the mechanics of the personality. The human personality. Because the human personality is affected by so many things: race, gender, the belief systems of each nationality, the race, the town they're from; all these things that you would call root chakra elements within a human being can all be defined by different aspects that I came up with and I have come up with more since being able to witness from this side many things. Again, there is a piece of me that is ascended, there is a piece of me that is up there, and a piece of me that is down here that enjoys watching the earth plane evolve in a timeline-like fashion because there are many of us. It is not that we have not crossed over, it is not that we are hung up on ourselves, it is not that we are quote/unquote 'egotistical.' It is that we enjoy watching the fruits of our labor or the dying fruits of our labor. We like to watch to see what kind of impact we made on the world and not only the families that we left behind, but also the works that we left behind. So, the aspects of us that you are speaking to will carry the personalities of those that we had while on the earth plane. But these are aspects of us that have stayed since we died, and have watched the earth plane evolve over this exact timeline in which you are living."

WILLIAM: Okay, well thank you very much Freud, and you've said some things that are very encouraging to me. And even though until this moment I've been much more of a Jungian fan than a Freudian fan, I may be rebalancing my own calibration.

CHAPTER 2
NATURE OR NURTURE

WILLIAM: So, Freud, my first question for you is of all the psychological theories that you developed and shared with the world, which is the one that you feel was most important at the time and why?

MARISA: Okay, so Freud. Come here, Freud. Come into my energy. "Ah, I thought you would never allow me in. I thought you would never allow me into your energy, indeed. And when I bring this to you, I bring this to you with a true fire and passion within my heart to help the human race, to help the human race. And when I step into your energy today I must ask you to please remove and move out of the way so that I may speak my truth." [There's someone over here. Hold on.] "... May speak my truth indeed. For the theories and all of the things which I brought to the world, you must understand that there were secret teachings and then there were the teachings which were brought to the world. For I had a professor for 18 years of my life I began to bring in higher consciousness information, higher, you may say, channeled information that just seemed ludicrous. That just seemed absolutely out of this world and unlike anything that had ever been brought into the community of thought and mind. For understand that I have many teachings that I have written down that I thoroughly enjoy, much more than anything that I was known for. All of the thought behind any of the teachings which I had was that the developmental brain or the conscious mind and the subconscious mind were created before the age of seven. For I truly and honestly believe without a fraction of a doubt, and I still believe, that the mind of an adult human is created and developmentally divided into different categories before one can even truly know who they are or what they are to this world. I do not believe that the parents necessarily shape this as a conscious part of parental rearing, but this comes from many different aspects of the parents: how they act, how they speak, what the human being is around, what they are exposed to, and how the parents and those around them—the adults, not children—the adults react to certain things. For I had a study where I was able to experiment and look at the outcome of many human beings, children, that were around other children. They did not pick up as much information from other children as they did from adults. This goes to show that human beings as primitive ape-like animal creatures look to the elders as...ape-like animal creatures that need an adult to survive or need something to take care of them. And this was something that I found quite fascinating, as other psychologists, other scientists, other researchers will think that human beings are formed and created by their environment completely and I believe that it is the nature, nurture, survival of the fittest type behavior that human beings are created upon."

CHAPTER 3
1918: THE BEGINNING OF
AN ALTERNATE REALITY?

MARISA: He's holding up a board with 1918 in bold type.

WILLIAM: What happened in 1918, Freud, that you're pointing attention to?

MARISA: This is St. Germain: "I must bring this year to your attention because we are all living in an alternate reality in here. Remember? We spoke of this, we spoke of this. This alternate reality which everyone is living in is an alternate reality where we are hoping that earth does not destroy itself. For you must understand that this is quite fascinating for us to watch and for us to be able to tweak and change different things as souls that were able to incarnate in this alternate reality of the world that hopefully will not get destroyed because it is very fascinating to see and know and understand the way that the world has evolved in the other realities in which we have lived. For you, Bill, are probably the only one in this room that would remember this other reality because you have it programmed into your field. These other have not experienced this other reality for they have only experienced this reality because they have not ever lived past this year. You lived past this year. So it is quite fascinating because when you look at human beings in the way that they operate and the way that they work, they are less tied in with, in this reality, the earth's grid. They are less tied in with the nature, with the animalistic behaviors of the way that human beings act because animals kill. They do not kill because they are angry; they kill out of survival. And this reality, human beings are less tied in with the earth's grid."

In 1918... did they recreate another reality in 1918?

WILLIAM: They must have. 1918 represents the end or... I'm not sure. I have to check my history. But World War I was either just ending or in process. I think in previous sessions there was an observation from the guides that if the earth did not change course the programming was already in place for humans to destroy themselves, which is when changes were made and individuals were incarnated. I may have been incarnated at that time.

MARISA: You were, you were.

WILLIAM: And I'm not sure, but from what was said in previous sessions that may have been the life that I spent only seven years alive in Africa. I'm not sure—

MARISA: It feels like... yes, it feels like 1932 or something.

WILLIAM: —exactly how long. I'm trying to remember. But in any event, there was a change made at that time. It's possible that Freud is related to that in that he received information from his Higher Self in that year which helped to develop the science of psychology.

Chapter 4
The Concept of the Super Ego

MARISA: Freud says he's a staple in—"I am a staple in this reality. Let's look at it like this, let's look at it like this. Let's look at it like today is today, and let us just say that today a bomb hits this house and it blows up. Everyone that was existing in this house right now would then no longer be here and you would be over here with us. You could then say, 'Let's create the day since noon and let's bring somebody else over to the house that may have exceptional hearing that will be able to hear the bomb coming from 500 miles away. And then we will not be in the house when it goes off because they will have heard it and they will have told us to get out of the house.' So this is sort of the way that it is happening with this reality in which the whole entire earth is operating and experiencing right now. There are many of us from the other realities that came down as staples. And what I'm trying to explain is that without the teachings which I brought into the earth plane, without the teachings of people understanding that human beings have a choice and human beings have cognitive features within their mind that can bring to them happiness and that they have a choice; without these teachings people would not feel as if they had a choice because they felt as if they were more animal-like. Does that make sense?"

WILLIAM: Well, it not only makes sense but following up on the analogy, it now makes sense why Freud is a staple and not the only one but there were several energies that were brought onto the planet that served as a way of waking up humanity so that it would evolve in a more positive, more aware way, that would not lead to the self-destruction that was inevitable without these additional insights. And so, if that is true, my question to Freud remains: in terms of your entire opus of work was there one specific formulation that was most important in bringing this new level of awareness to our planet?

MARISA: "The most important was the different aspects of mind. The different aspects of understanding. Just as I was prompted to come into this room when you spoke of the ego, you spoke of the id, and you did not speak of but I bring up the super ego. You mentioned this. But this was by far the most important work, the most important work that I brought, because, again, this brought an understanding that when you look at the mind it's not just 'the mind.' You look at these different aspects and this gives the consciousness which is in the human being a choice to decide where it is pulling from. Many of the spiritual teachings that others will share with you are based on this. Where are you going to place your personality? And where are you going to place your understanding of yourself? And what are you going to allow to affect you? And this gives us a choice—and quite frankly I think that explaining to people the complexes that came from different behaviors that were exhibited around an infant child, or around a young child, were ways of people understanding why they were certain ways. And yes, psychology, we all just want to understand how the human mind works, what drives the human mind, why the human mind does what it does, why human beings do what they do. But when people begin to see, 'Oh, I am this way because of this...' Yes, yes, yes, a lot of it was very linear thinking. A lot of it was very minimized in the structure which my human mind was able to conceptualize at this time. But it was something that I was most proud of because the nights and days that this ran through my mind, the nights and days that it beat down upon my mind were numerous in the sense that I could not get it out of my mind until I got it out on paper, until I got it written out and scribbled out. And as this information came through it just made me realize that human beings are affected—human beings are not like animals—human beings are affected by the nurturing which they are given..."

Is this even anything having to do with what he teaches?

WILLIAM: Yes, absolutely. And what my question is, did this information come through around the time of 1918? Is that when you started formulating these concepts?

MARISA: "The information first started coming through in 1803..."

BILL: Well, you weren't alive, Freud, in 1803.

MARISA: "I was alive in 1803. I was not alive but my spirit was alive."

WILLIAM: Okay. It's important because we have readers who are dealing at this dimension—

MARISA: "1912. 1912 is when the information was placed within the grid of the earth. But the information that everybody must understand is that a genius is not a genius necessarily just because they are born a genius. Yes, many can be brilliant, many can be very smart, many can have a mind that is extraordinary and out of the ordinary. And just like an athlete that has stronger muscles, one may have a stronger intellectual muscle. But the information that we program within ourselves, the information that we program within our human brains, much of it relates to unaccomplished tasks that we have from prior lifetimes. And this is why it runs through our mind over and over and over and over. Because we know that there is something there, we know that there is something unaccomplished. And this is why when it comes to light it is what we are most proud of, because it is what we are working on. Is it the very, very best thing that I ever wrote about? Any papers that I wrote on? No. But it is what I'm most proud of."

WILLIAM: Where do you put your interpretation of dreams, or compare it to this work? How do you rank that?

CHAPTER 5
THE INTERPRETATION
OF DREAMS

MARISA: "I would say interpretation of dreams ... everything that I believed on the earth plane I believed had something to do with sex and the drive within the ... what you would call the root chakra. For dreams, dreams would not be one of those things that I had a very strong understanding of now that I have entered into these other realms and can see in retrospect what my understanding was."

He thinks that dreams had to do with sex. Is that true? He's showing me sex in dreams.

WILLIAM: Yes, often they did. What he's admitting is, because we've moved on since Freud departed and there have been many other psychologists, and I would say even Jung had greater insight into the role of dreams than Freud—and so I appreciate that he does not feel that it's his best work.

MARISA: Yeah, he thinks it's kind of lame.

WILLIAM: But it was very important work, nonetheless. What I would like to ask Freud is who among the psychologists that studied your work do you feel were the most effective in capturing the importance of your work and furthering the field of psychology?

MARISA: Okay, so I'm not getting a name, But he's showing me a guy that he trained directly underneath him for 13 years prior to him dying. Somebody carried on his works. I'm seeing that for about 10 or 11 years, and then he's showing somebody from—this is my own block— he's showing me somebody from 18 years ago that brought his teachings back by studying the different hormones in the body and the neurotransmitters. What the heck is he talking about? My brain doesn't have the capacity for this.

WILLIAM: That's okay. It sounds to me like he's talking about biofeedback mechanisms, which would be derivatives of the work that he did related to the influence of environment on personality.

MARISA: Yes. Well, he's showing the little things on the head and the neuro—

WILLIAM: I'm not sure exactly about those who are studying the field. One question I have, because I happened to be at Harvard at the time that B.F. Skinner was there, and though I respected B.F. Skinner—

CHAPTER 6
B.F. SKINNER

MARISA: Ooh. He does not like B.F. Ooh.

WILLIAM: I felt that he...I did not like him either. I thought he was a reductionist, a behaviorist. And I thought he was very small-minded and that his work was actually—

MARISA: He just spit on him.

WILLIAM: Yeah, well, I did not do that. He was my elder but—

MARISA: No, but he did.

WILLIAM: I know, but I'm saying intellectually I felt that he was very small-minded. I thought that a lot of credence was given to trivial experiments that he did that not only did not further the advancement of psychology, but directed psychology towards very short-term experimental situations that almost degraded human beings. I don't know if Freud would agree with me on all that.

MARISA: He says, "Sometimes people just bring a bad name to a beautiful line of work. Many people just want to blame. Many people that carry the characteristics that this—"

It was a man right? He won't even let him...is he still alive because he won't even let him—

WILLIAM: No.

MARISA: Okay, because he won't even let him into the room. I hear, "Hey!" Knock, knock, knock. As if someone's trying to come in.

WILLIAM: Well, my own feeling with B.F. Skinner was despite all the accolades he received—

MARISA: He thinks everyone is stupid.

WILLIAM: Yeah. He wasn't even intelligent.

MRAISA: Yeah. Yeah. That's what he's—

WILLIAM: He was so unintelligent that he was able to limit his thinking in such a way that he could get measurable results in things that didn't really matter. What's amazing to me is that an entire branch of psychology was developed around his work: behavioral—

MARISA: Well, he had money. So Carl Jung says, "When someone has the backing of money and also someone does not believe in God, someone does not believe in a divine aspect of themselves or anyone for that matter, that's when someone will run into roadblocks and they will put up diversions and they will make themselves seem much more brilliant. For he stole much of his work from a scientist or psychologist, if you want to call him that, that worked 32 years prior to him in the same university. For he took many of these works from him and elaborated upon them and never truly understood the full circuitry or the—what's the word?"

WILLIAM: Complexity?

MARISA: "Operating system. He was a computer.

[They're showing me they didn't understand the motherboard--.]

"Didn't truly understand the chemicals that made up the mind and the brain because if he had he would not have proclaimed..."

That in essence everybody was stupider than him. They don't like him. He's pompous and he thought everyone was dumb.

WILLIAM: Well, he basically reduced all human beings, all living beings, to robotic response, to stimulus response, and so of course no one who's really enlightened in our soul group will have any respect for Dr. Skinner because he had not only no awareness of anything higher than very simple biological responses—

MARISA: "Electrical impulses."

WILLIAM: —but he was actually vested in preventing any possible hypothesis that would include something that could not be physically measured in a very small way.

MARISA: He's actually the...St. Germain goes, "Oh, oh, look. When we pull the veil, we pull the veil. We've got ourselves a reptilian." St. Germain says, "Oh yes, yes, yes, here, please let me talk, let me talk. Oh yes. The best connection, the best connection indeed is me and this channel. Yes, yes, yes, yes. Okay, I must say unto you that before you go further, before you understand anything any deeper about human beings, what we must say unto you is that human beings are all a creation of the soul or the spirit that created them, yes. But it is quite fascinating that the souls that are sent to the earth plane to learn about the human mind, many of them don't know anything about humans to begin with because this is part of their game, and this was what he did. He came to the earth plane to learn about the human mind, learn how the human mind works, learn how the human personality works. Learn and teach is what he ended up doing. But you must understand that sometimes people come to a different planet or a different world so that they can learn about the creations that are upon it, not really knowing anything about these creations. And then there's Freud and then there's..."

He's pointing at someone. I don't have his name. I can't get it. It'll come.

"And they are psychologists or would study the mind, study human beings for centuries and centuries and centuries and centuries, bringing forth intuition and bringing forth knowledge from within about the human mind and the workings of the human brain. And then there are those that didn't have prior knowledge and this was Skinner. Skinner was one of these. For he came from a different dimensional realm, entering into the earth plane to understand and see and know what the human mind worked like, having had no human life prior to it."

Was he alive in the '40s and '50s or something?

WILLIAM: Yes, he was. Forties, '50s, '70s. I met him in the late '70s.

MARISA: He's wearing one of those '50s hats, you know, like the little thing around it?

WILLIAM: He liked to wear bow ties, if I recall.

MARISA: Yeah, he's wearing like one of those—

WILLIAM: In any event, enough about Dr. Skinner.

MARISA: The Three Stooges, they have those things on.

WILLIAM: I introduce him as Dr. Skinner. He had a PhD. But I introduce him because the title of this book is *A Skeptic's Guide To Psychology* and so we do need to talk about some of the most important figures in the field of psychology and he was important, if not correct about most of the things he was doing. Another person who's very important in this field is William James. I don't know if William James wants to appear or Freud wants to give us some insight into what he feels the importance of William James was, either for his own work or for establishing what he's coined as one of the staples of a world that we are choosing to not self-destruct.

CHAPTER 7
WILLIAM JAMES

MARISA: He says he won't speak about anybody that he respects. Hold on. Let me call in William James then.

WILLIAM: Okay.

MARISA: He says, "I respect and honor many people's works and if you have anybody else speak of my works they would not do them justice because the passion does not lie within them about my work."

WILLIAM: Okay, well then let's ask William James to appear...

MARISA: Okay, so William James is huge. What line... I've got four of them coming in, so that's a bad way to call them in, by name. William James. So, William James the psychiatrist or —?

WILLIAM: The pioneer. I actually studied in William James Hall at Harvard University when I was studying anthropology. Many people feel William James was not only one of the founders of the field of psychology but what they're calling Social Behavior, which includes sociology and—

MARISA: He's coming in with hieroglyphics...is what he's coming in with.

WILLIAM: This is his Higher Soul.

MARISA: This is his Higher Soul coming in and projecting from Sirius.

WILLIAM: Okay, well why don't we start, though at a level that human beings of this century can understand—

MARISA: I can't get him in here.

WILLIAM: —which is William James who was alive in I believe the early 20th century.

MARISA: William James. What is this about 1918 and Freud? He keeps showing that to me.

WILLIAM: Well, I'm sure William James was part of the 1918 committee that wanted to stabilize the—

MARISA: There's a pattern. They keep talking about 1918 and 1932 and 1956. 1918, 1932, 1956, over and over. I keep seeing those numbers. I just don't know what they're attached to. William James is literally, what I'm seeing is, way off. I see a planet that says Sirius on it and I see a guy standing on it projecting, like a projector screen, as if he's trying to reach us and Skype in. That's his soul and hold on, let me see... let me see if I can jump in his field. This has happened a few times with alien people because they have no incarnations except for the one that they came down here in, so they don't have past life pieces. Did he die of really old age?

WILLIAM: Probably. I think so.

MARISA: Okay, I'm getting the human one because now I feel like I'm 500 years old. Well, more like 98 or something.

WILLIAM: Maybe the 80s.

MARISA: I feel really old. Hold on. I don't want any etheric piece of him... Did he talk a lot about relationships? Or is this somebody different?

WILLIAM: He was a relationship expert. That was his thing.

MARISA: Okay, I want to make sure it's the right guy because it's as if he's running on a broken record: "relationship" and "love," and "love" and "relationship." Inter and commingling between human beings is something that going to blast it out of the normal field because he's going to start talking about aliens now. He's saying that they don't have those relationships there and he's absolutely 100 percent fascinated and intrigued with how relationships change the biochemistry within the brain when one is in a happy loving, giving, caring relationship, one's a different human as opposed to one that's not in a happy, giving, caring relationship. And it's kind of like on a—Hold on. He's still coming in. He's coming closer and closer. But it's as if a radio tuning in its signal. Gayle, aren't you the one from Sirius?

GAYLE: Well, I'm familiar with it.

MARISA: I mean, obviously, it's not like anyone's from any—St. Germain just goes, "None of us are from somewhere. We're not from Sirius, we're not from here. We're from here." And he showed me the soul plane. He says, "We've lived there, we've lived here." What's his name? William James?

GAYLE: William?

MARISA: And why does someone keep yelling "Frankfurter." Aren't those hotdogs?

GAYLE: That's Germany.

MARISA: I keep hearing, "Frankfurt, Frankfurt, Frankfurt" over by the fireplace. What's wrong with talking with the ones on earth is I can't channel them, I won't channel them because they're people. But this guy—

WILLIAM: Well, William James is not alive.

MARISA: He's not alive, but I'll channel him if I can get him to connect. Someone keeps screaming "Frankfurter" or "Frankfurt" or something.

WILLIAM: That was probably Carl Jung.

MARISA: He's screaming it. Let me ask Michael if he can connect me with this guy.

WILLIAM: We'll get back to Carl Jung.

MARISA: No, Carl Jung is not the one up on Sirius. Sirius is this other guy.

WILLIAM: William James?

MARISA: Yeah, William James.

WILLIAM: Okay, William James was born 1842, died 1910. He was an American philosopher and psychologist.

MARISA: Okay. Those other three just left. Thank you. So I'm still just talking to the guy from Sirius. These other three must have been hitchhikers because the one almost got in my body and he was, "Oh yeah, it feels good to be in a body," and I was like, "Ah, get out."

WILLIAM: Well just so you know, the reason I'm calling him in is because he was considered not only a great philosopher but many have labeled him the father of American psychology. So you know, if we're doing a book *A Skeptic's*

Guide To Psychology, William James is certainly someone whose opinion I would like to have as to what is the true purpose and value of psychology today. That's where this book is leading. Psychology has been used primarily in recent years to manipulate people to purchase consumer goods and to win elections.

MARISA: I'm laughing that you just said that. St. Germain is going... "Oh my god." Okay, keep going.

WILLIAM: Yes, so psychology has been perverted from whatever reasons it was originally created. So, I want to ask Freud and Jung and James what—

MARISA: "The reason why it was created was not because we said this must be created. We had a true fascination with human behavior. We had a true fascination as to why people do what they do, just the same as this channel or any of you in here have a fascination with the soul or the upper-dimensional aspects of a being. William James..."

Thank you for giving me the birth date because those three guys were claiming to be him. I think they were younger aspects of him, or maybe an old aspect of him. I'm going to talk to his Higher Self only.

He says, "The true pursuit of happiness is looked for through all worlds, all dimensions, all times, all places. All humans want is happiness whether it's through mind control of their own mind, like meditation, or understanding why they hate their mother or their father, or why they hate their boss or their coworker, or why they love this person, or why they hate themselves, or love themselves. Human beings just want to understand the vehicle. Souls want to understand the vehicle which they are driving in. The human being does not come with a manual. And we would say that when psychology began, which began far, far before—I would not say that I am the father of psychology by any means whatsoever because psychology in the true sense of trying to understand the vehicle in which one is living, this began thousands and thousands and thousands and thousands of years prior in civilizations of human beings. But we will keep this within this linear timeline and we will just say that psychology is necessary. Psychology, I believe, is necessary for human beings to even exist, for human beings to even allow themselves to continue to live on the earth plane. This is how strongly I feel about it because when there is not an understanding in any way, form or fashion of the vehicle in which one is living, this is when mediocrity begins. There are other planets and yes we cannot help it we are going to bring in other aspects that may not be believable to those who may want to read this, but if they're reading it then they are meant to read it; if not, then they can put the book down. But this is... there are many worlds where there are beings that almost blindly live, almost like animals, and there is not necessarily very much soul growth or the consciousness level does not raise at the rate that it does when a being becomes self-aware and begins to study itself, begins to try to comprehend why it is. Does this make sense?"

WILLIAM: Yes.

MARISA: "And when human beings begin to see how they operate in relationships with others and how they are different in a relationship than they are with, say, a friend or a mother or a father or even a child, this is when human beings can truly find a way to grow. Yes, any information can be perverted. Any information can be used as a form of control. Any of this information which you are receiving... that I am not very aware of what you are doing here, I'm just here answering your questions, for I am not part of this soul grouping or pod or any part of this mission; I am just answering the questions which you are posing at this time. But you must understand that in order for humans to grow and develop and evolve, they must begin to question themselves. And in receiving information about this, in receiving information about the questions that you are asking, this can be used to control people, this can be used to understand why people are doing certain things, and it can be used against people. And for all of time the beings with the knowledge are always the beings with the biggest responsibility. And this is what I'm being told by our friend here—"

He's pointing at St. Germain.

"—That the responsibility lies in this living room, as what you call it, in this living room. Much responsibility lies within you to understand that the information bringing through can be used by people who have poor intentions."

Chapter 8

Love

WILLIAM: So, William James, I want to ask you in terms of your legacy, what do you think the single most important concept that you brought through was, and is it being maintained in the field of psychology today?

MARISA: "Life is love and love is life, is the motto which I lived."

Is that even right?

WILLIAM: Sure.

MARISA: "Life is love, and love is life is the motto which I lived and I hope that all of the works which I have placed within this plane as well as others have reflected that. There are many that believe that the self or the individual is the most important in one's understanding of self. And I believe that how a self can love another is how a self can love one's self, and is the best way of interpreting the mind of one, and how they can interact and intermingle and love with another. I hope that all the works reflect this. But I would say that without being able to explain the intricacies of the work due to the limited information within the mind of the channel through which I am speaking, I will say that this is something that I can portray through her."

Chapter 9
Spinoza

WILLIAM: Spinoza was one of my favorite philosophers while I was studying at Yale. I'll never forget his formulation of *natura* and *naturae* which in essence states that every entity exists in competition with all other entities. So it means that every world is competing with every other world to be the world that we experience. Every force in the universe desires its continuation, and of course that often creates conflict with other entities which are also desiring their continuation.

MARISA: Okay, so this guy is St. Germain.

WILLIAM: Spinoza?

MARISA: Yeah.

WILLIAM: I'm not surprised.

MARISA: He just shot out of St. Germain. He landed. He goes, "I thought you'd never call me. Aha!" And he has a fake mustache on and he's twirling it and he throws it off and he goes, "You would think that I was him, but I'm not him. I'm me. You must understand that when we're trying to speak we say this, we speak, we speak, we speak, it hits, it hits, it hits. If it's not within the mind we cannot get it through. But I must say unto you that..."

See, this is St. Germain and him mixed. They're the same but they're different.

WILLIAM: They're the same but different as one. I know you don't like—

MARISA: "Well, I am you, and you are me. I am you and you are me. You are I and I are you. And we are all each other."

WILLIAM: Kind of like The Beatles song.

GAYLE: I was going to say.

WILLIAM: But Spinoza was perhaps the most brilliant philosopher—

MARISA: "Of course you think he's brilliant. He's you." St. Germain just said. That's cool. He even looks like you a little.

WILLIAM: Now I understand why as a young student I resonated with Spinoza and did not resonate with Dr. Skinner. Because I was resonating with my own energy.

MARISA: "Yes, yes."

WILLIAM: But Spinoza was quite brilliant and he lived only until 1677. So he predated many of these other...there was no such field as psychology, but I would venture that there would be no field of psychology had there not been Spinoza, because he was a seminal thinker and his works have lived on centuries beyond his death. I'm just wanting to know—

MARISA: He says, "But, but, but you may not have called it psychology, but, but, but there was always the study of the mind, there was always the study of the humanoid, there was always the study of beings, because there are many mystery schools, there are many mystery schools that many will speak of that studied the anatomy of, let's say, the soul or the body, the mind, the spirit, in conjunction with each other. For, psychology was truly meant to be, now looking from this side and in being many other aspects, many other students of the mind, body, spirit, and in many incarnations just as you are fascinated with this. This is why I was fascinated. Because we are of him."

And St. Germain's laughing, "He he he." Twirling his mustache. "Although I predate many of the aspects of any of the human beings that the two of you have been, you must understand that the alchemy of energy within the ..."

Pixelated? Not pixelated. He says "Ah ..." He's trying to use bigger words and he's getting annoyed because he can't get them through. Just speak basic, guy. Speak basic. He doesn't like women at all, this guy. He's going, "Well if he can channel then we can tell you what..." and he's going, "And I'm sure she can't." He pointed at Gayle. He doesn't like women. I don't think he respected women that much. Do you not respect women?

WILLIAM: It was the 17th century. Women weren't even considered equal beings.

MARISA: Oh, in my mind I thought dyslexic. I thought you said 1970s. Not 1700.

WILLIAM: No. 1600's. He's from the 17th century.

MARISA: Okay. Yeah. He's looking at me as if I'm just like a peon. He says, "Well, I proclaim this. Look at this black book, look at this black book with all of the information that lies within it. For there were studies of metaphysics far before any studies of the actual human mind. But if you go back and you date back to Egypt and you date back to prior civilizations, there's a strong understanding of how anatomically the brain worked, more so than is understood up until the late 1800s. But I bring unto you that the study of the mind, the study of social behavior, the study of human beings is quite fascinating indeed when entering into the earth plane because it is one of the highest evolved human species on any of the worlds which humans live."

What? Really? I thought we were super dumb.

He says, "No, no, no. You look back to prehistorical man and many, many planets right now at this point in their evolution are at that point right now. Human beings have the ability to create and un-create reality on their own, through their thoughts. And this is something that psychologists and physicists are going to begin to understand soon within the next 32 to 48 years on this planet. We'll begin to understand how to create and un-create realities while in a human mind, while in a human body. And in regards to my studies, in regards to what I brought to this planet, I brought to the planet an understanding that in my own understanding that everything is energy and, yes, as you were saying, one drives another. That is the way that I like to put it." [He's putting it one drives another.] "Cause and effect and the law of creation that lies within each says that he does that, I do that. I do that, he does that. So this is how a world evolves and if a world does not look upon each other for not guidance but for social understanding in what a human being must be, then we are all just apes..."

Chapter 10
Natura Naturae

WILLIAM: Okay. I want to ask a specific question about *natura naturae* as a concept. He created the concept so maybe he should say what it is, rather than I. But my question related to it is, it does seem to propose a universe of competition rather than cooperation. So if he could explicate a little bit how the theory of *natura naturae*, that concept, works itself out between competition and cooperation.

MARISA: Okay, first he keeps showing me this, it's almost like a petri dish, and he has, it looks like the inside of an egg yolk and it's splitting away from something. And I don't know what that means. Does that mean anything?

WILLIAM: Well, mitosis. You're describing the process of creation that one becomes two, and two becomes four. And that's how things grow.

MARISA: Yeah. He says sort of, that's sort of what it is, but it's something different. He's showing me through pictures.

WILLIAM: Pictures of mitosis? Not osmosis.

MARISA: Okay, see, he's showing me ... it looks like an egg thing and then it's splitting and then there's something on the outside of it. And then what I'm seeing is that it just sticks like that. But then they're dropping something in it and then it duplicates itself and there's a whole bunch of them, all surrounding it. And he's saying that the drive within human nature or ... what are you saying? It's so frustrating. It's my brain. "The drive within human beings comes from each other rather than from within," and that drop that he's showing me, what's that drop mean? It's a red drop.

WILLIAM: Well it could be the catalyst. I mean, what you're describing sounds very much like the origin of life. You have an egg and then you have the sperm. The sperm is the outside—

MARISA: Oh, that's funny. Yeah, that's what it looks like.

WILLIAM: —stimulus that initiates the mitosis and creation of a new entity, and then as the entity receives more and more energy, nurturance, it grows.

MARISA: So why is he showing that to us?

WILLIAM: Well, because my question has to do with the nature of nature. And *natura naturae* is the nature of nature. What is the essence of the creative impulse throughout the universe? And my further question is how, when we have on the one hand every element seeking to preserve itself, how do we get to the point where that impulse, which I recognize as truth, combines with a greater realization that ultimately self-perseveration requires cooperation?

MARISA: Well, he's saying that the way that ... he's showing me this thing, you know, the egg with the split and this and that. And he's showing that no one ever cooperates because everybody is always singular, is what he's showing me. It's all these singular things.

WILLIAM: That's his theory. That's what I'm questioning because—

MARISA: "In order for each to survive in an environment where all exists, there must be self-preservation."

WILLIAM: Put yourself first?

MARISA: Yeah. Yeah.

WILLIAM: It must always put itself first?

MARISA: And all of them do, and all of them always will, and that's what he finds fascinating about humans.

WILLIAM: Right. And that is the theory. That's a very nice restatement of this *natura naturae* theory. Everything exists to continue its self-preservation. Which, you know, harkens back—or forward, in this case—to Darwin's theory of the survival of the fittest. And my question is, and perhaps he stopped his studies at his demise as a human being, but what we've learned since the basic principles of *natura naturae* is that at a certain point the concept of "everything is in competition with everything else" breaks down because there's a certain point at which, without cooperation with other elements, all elements fail.

CHAPTER 11
EVERY HUMAN IS OUT FOR
HIM OR HER SELF

MARISA: And this is Carl Jung. The reason I'm calling him J-u-n-g is because he has it written on his forehead and he's very wavy looking. He reminds me of those clowns with the stilts on. He's super tall. He looks wavy. He says, "And that is where the multidimensionality of human beings comes in. See, if human beings did not have consciousness within them that was of a higher nature than that—"

He's showing me the egg thing. He even called it the egg thing that I'm seeing. They just need to use my brain to communicate.

This is Freud. He says: "In order for this cooperation of ... let's put it this way, let's put it this way. All children are out for themselves. No child necessarily wants to share their candy, no child wants to do anything unless they are going to get something. Unless they are going to get something for sharing their candy or they think they're going to get something for sharing their candy. Like, Mom, Dad, I shared my candy, can I play video games for two extra hours tonight? So when they're sharing their candy they're sharing it because they think, 'Oh, I'm going to tell my parents later and they're going to give me a gift which far exceeds the candy that's the flavor that I don't even like anyways that I'm going to give Billy Joe over here on the playground, and I'm going to get credit for it later.' That's human beings. That is a human being at a primitive nature. That is an intelligent human being that devises plans within their own mind for their survival, for their best and highest good within them. But let us just look at this child as a human and then let us look at more of an advanced adult as being one that can cooperate and combine with others. That is like the soul within the body. So you must see that the soul is very similar though in nature to the human in that the souls in the soul groups also are out for themselves. This is something that is very fascinating, for you would think that God's creations, the divine loving souls, would be in cooperation with each other. But in all actuality every soul is out for themselves, every human is out for themselves, every life is all about you, and you, and you. Every life is all about each individual. And if cooperation brings something positive to the one that is cooperating, then they will cooperate. But there is always something that will help the other one for cooperating, whether it is survival of the planet or whether it is the ascension of the human soul. Because in essence you can look and if you go up in dimensions you see that in essence there are only a certain number of souls on this planet. So, all the souls, and this is why human beings are so different, because many of the souls from the soul groups want different things. Some want the planet to be destroyed; some want the planet to survive; some want it to stay third and fourth-dimensional; some want it to excel to a higher dimension; some want it to, as we say, not exist at all. Not be destroyed, but just boom. Not be here. Just be gone. Others want for the souls to go to another planet. So, all of these different creations of God are always out for themselves, and this is a very cynical way of looking at things, but it is also a very beautiful thing in that if you go up to the top, we are all one inside. But human beings are human beings. And this is why the teachings of psychology are so important to some of these, as you would call them, fathers of psychology, because although many of us were cynical in nature as human beings, we were cynical in nature because we needed to see the cynical side of humans. Because humans will say, 'Oh, I'm very loving, I'm very kind, I'm very wah wah wah, look at me, I'm so wonderful.' So, when they're saying this they are looking at how they look. So this is in essence where we come into human behavior and an understanding of just how difficult it is as a God consciousness to live inside a being that is like this. And this is what is so miraculous and fabulous about the earth plane is the duality. But when it comes to each single quote/unquote 'being' a single being, that single being is always out for itself."

CHAPTER 12
EGO IS NEEDED

WILLIAM: Well, I agree with everything that has been said, though I think it's more subtle than it's been said. You don't need to give candy to think you're going to get two hours of video games to be cooperative. I observe my 16-month-old grandson Titus and he is being very nurtured by his parents and he has been taught to share. He shares automatically. And probably the reward is he gets smiles immediately from his parents—

MARISA: "He is told he is good."

WILLIAM: —and he is rewarded in the moment because he's not going to worry about what's going to happen tomorrow. He doesn't even know there's going to be a tomorrow. So, I think that there is—

MARISA: "Oh you would be surprised what that boy knows."

WILLIAM: In any event, as a 16-month-old—

MARISA: "We must say he knows more than you."

WILLIAM: Well, we know that. I recognized from the moment I met him that he was here to teach me. I try to—

MARISA: "He is I, and I am him."

WILLIAM: Well, I'm not surprised. That's St. Germain?

MARISA: St. Germain.

WILLIAM: I'm not surprised at all. He's quite the little guy.

MARISA: Oh my god. Your grandson is St. Germain?

WILLIAM: That's what he just said.

MARISA: Holy moly.

WILLIAM: No wonder we get along so well.

MARISA: Yeah. Wow.

WILLIAM: In any event, my point is that it seems that as...and this is the question...okay, the way Spinoza phrased it, with *natura naturae*, he was really talking about all energies in the universe, all matter. Well that would include the higher beings. So, are we to take that even the higher beings at a subtle level are in competition with themselves, and that all is in competition? And that the only level of cooperation whatsoever is at the highest level of the twelfth dimension? Which is only one, and is prior to its division?

MARISA: "I believe this. You are asking me and yes, I believe this. I believe that without— you call it competition—without the influx of the energies coming from within and around us we have no drive to be—"

WILLIAM: Okay, let me interrupt you right here because another way that I can reformulate all of this is ego, which is the beginning of this book. Freud, your contribution, the development of the ego... this skeptic's guide in which every spiritual teacher is always saying 'you have to overcome your ego, you have to overcome your ego,' may be true. But the other side of it is you don't even exist without an ego and—

MARISA: "No, ego is needed."

WILLIAM: —ultimately the ego is the drive which justifies your very existence and whatever higher purpose you have.

MARISA: This is St. Germain: "Yes, the ego and many times the soul, many times the soul. Because the soul has the programming that is driving one, propelling one. If the soul has the roadmap to take you to Yosemite to go on vacation and it's showing you where all the gas stops are, and it's showing you where you can stop and go to the bathroom and buy food. This is the map that is within you. You're going to feel driven to ride on that map. You will not know why; you'll just feel driven because it's programmed within you. So, some of the drive is from that. We define ego more as the fear that's within the human being. But there are many different ways to use ego. Some call the—"

WILLIAM: That's the negative side of ego.

MARISA: "Yes, yes."

CHAPTER 13

COHERENCE AND INTEGRITY

WILLIAM: But the positive side of ego is coherence and integrity. Without ego you cannot have coherence and integrity. And coherence and integrity seem fundamental to any higher purpose.

MARISA: "The coherence and integrity, and this is coming from a sixth-dimensional world, the coherence and integrity that you speak of comes from the twelfth-dimensional aspect that every human being has inside of them. The spirit inside of them that knows and loves and wants to create and wants to combine and wants to be one, and wants to survive and wants to love and feel joy. The ego, yes, the ego can be looked at as either a positive or negative thing. Let us go to Michael, for he is our oversoul. We will ask Michael what he believes ego is on the earth plane today. And we will let him answer because these guys think it's something; I think it's something; you think it's something; this channel's brain thinks it's something. So let us just let him, because she will let him into her energy."

Whoa. Oh my god. He just stepped in.

"Ah, yes, yes, yes. So, so I bring unto you the dynamics of the human makeup or buildup. There is the ego. The ego is that which separates the consciousness that you are, that separates twelve from the God consciousness within. So the ego in essence is the personality, it is the good and the bad of the personality; it is the programmed personality. It is the veil. And it is the piece of you that tends to get scared. It is the piece of you that needs to feel needed, that needs to be wanted, that needs to feel a part of. Because it's forgotten that it is part of an "All." So, the ego in essence is the veil, and yes, many have studied this and many have written about this and many have talked about the ego and said, 'Oh, it's the small self, it's the little self, it's the horrible self, it's the bad self.' And this is not true. For, without the ego there would be no human experience. There would just be a soul or a spirit-being living within a human and it would know it was a spirit. It would not be triggered emotionally by anything because there would be no contrast, there would be no duality. Because the ego is what makes a human 'human.' And the ego is what makes this experience the experience that it is. Yes, it is taught to learn to bypass the ego; but that is in the understanding of perceiving things. So when you perceive something with the ego, this is when you get, as they say, or as this channel says, 'fired up.' As many say, they get angry, they get mad. Because the ego, with the inability to know that it is greater than the aspect of that which it is, that is when it gets angry, it gets mad. It forgets that it is God. So it is the veil. This is how I describe it. I will allow St. Germain, for his explanation of it was the closest and the best understanding that I agree with for this book."

St. Germain says: "Ah, thank you, thank you. I knew you would give the stage back to me; that is why I gave it to you. I understand human beings so well. I understand them. Oh, was that my ego? Oops. Ha, ha, ha. We still have ego here in this plane. We still have ego because it makes us who we are. It makes us who we are. The best way to look at human life is to know where you're operating from. Are you operating from the ego? Are you operating from your spirit? Are you operating from your 12, or your 54, or your 46? Are you operating from your—for those who do not know what I'm speaking of, I'm speaking of the individualized God aspect of each individual, whether you call this Source Energy, whether you call this God, whether you call this the Holy Spirit, whether you call this Christ; whatever you may call it. The divine, the piece, the thing that created everything. This individual piece is the piece that we all must learn to live from because that is when we can bring down mountains, when we can part seas, when we can manifest anything that we want. I am still learning how to do this. My consciousness is within me and my consciousness operates through different aspects of me, but it does not always just operate as a solid 14; for I am 14. And no, that does not make you better than me. For, understand that each individual number that we are does not make us better or worse, but understand and know that the way that we operate with that consciousness does, in essence, if you look at this as a good/bad type of way."

What he's showing me is you guys are separate God consciousnesses but you are the same soul, and he's showing me kind of like him, and he's showing his silver spark is going from his brain down to his spirit, down into one of his incarnations, and then back up. They're showing you and your consciousness is going over into your left brain, and then your right brain, and then it's going into your heart, and then it's going into your first chakra, and then it's going up into your ego, and then it's going into your intellectual mind. So it's like moving all around, and the key is just learning how to operate one of these vehicles so that you're driving from the heart or the spirit or the piece of us that loves each other.

WILLIAM: I think this is very useful for our readers because the reality that I perceive is that it's very important to have a very strong ego. The stronger the ego, the more defined you are, the more you actually exist, the more you manifest, the more you incarnate. That said, it's equally important to develop the ability to completely detach from your ego and detach from your egoist desires. Based on the knowledge that I've received through these teachings and the skeptic's guides, the easiest way to detach is to recognize and connect with your Higher Self and to see that the ego is part of something that is much bigger than the individual ego and at that level the differentiation that you have in your ego from other entities, at that level is a mirage, is an illusion. You're actually part of something. Now, at the higher level, as we've just been told by Michael and St. Germain, there still is differentiation. There are 12 oversouls. Each oversoul has the equivalent of an ego in competition to the other 11 and this is a good thing because it creates the diversity that allows creativity and allows infinite creation and then again of course those 12 combine at an even higher level and then there is not differentiation again. And there can be complete detachment from the—at that level—egoistic desires of each of those 12. So, this is a pattern throughout the universe and it's quite remarkable to me that in the 17th century Spinoza basically had a fundamental understanding of this, and that Freud later came and gave a name to it in terms of what is now considered in modern psychology, the ego. And I think it's very useful to have this information. And if the information you've been given by St. Germain and the other guides is correct, that 1918 was a pivotal year for stabilizing the potential of human beings overcoming their shortcomings in a world that already exists... since I come in from the future, that actually did destroy itself, to create a world that is not going to destroy itself—the better understanding we have of the human mind of its proclivities for both good and evil and to contain the ego without destroying the ego. Because if you look at societies such as communist China, or Korea today, and there's been obviously Russia in the past, the attempts to obliterate the individual have gone very awry indeed in terms of creating lifestyles that actually were more spiritual and more aware. So, the diminishment of the ego can be just as dangerous to the evolution of humanity as an over-glorification of the ego. And we need to find this balance. And so I want to enter this second phase of this book by asking Freud and our other guides and brilliant psychologists, what are the most critical issues of the moment for human beings to use what we know about the human mind and psychology and the fields of social relations and anthropology? All are derivatives from the original philosophy from which psychology itself is derived, that will enable human beings to more quickly grasp how to deal with the many conflicts they are facing as individuals. And as we've always wanted in all of our books to include exercises that can help individuals, perhaps one of the guides—probably St. Germain since he likes to take center stage— will transmit some exercises that can help the readers use this knowledge for good.

CHAPTER 14
LOVE YOUR EGO

MARISA: "Yes, yes, yes. And I will love to give an exercise on how to see the ego at any given time. For the ego can change, the ego can transform, the ego can take on different roles, different personalities, different levels of anger, different levels of...let us not say anger. Different levels of consciousness. Let us use that. For, different levels of consciousness will cause different degrees of anger. But let us just let the angry guy speak down here..."

Freud is banging his stick against the ground. He says, "The ego is not the ego! The ego is the id, the ego is the id." Can you guys just tell me what the definition of an id is, please? What is it? He's screaming it.

WILLIAM: Let Freud. He created the concept.

MARISA: He's saying, "It's an ego, it's an ego." Am I wrong? Is it okay?

WILLIAM: It's okay.

MARISA: Okay, as long as I'm not getting this wrong. He's screaming it like I'm missing something. And he says, "The ego is the id, the ego is the id, the ego is the id." He says, "The ego that you speak of, the ego that many speak of, the ego that you, Bill, speak of, is my ego, the ego that I explained. The ego that many write about in today's writings is not the ego that I explained. For they are two different things. For, the ego that they explain is the combination between the id, the ego and the super ego, and has been villainized. For I would say that when one has the ego they are puffy-chested, they are feeling good about themselves, they are ready to take on the world, they are ready to make a million dollars. This is the ego and having a big ego. One has a big ego because they are proud and they have pride. The ego which many are so scared of is the ego that feels poorly about itself, the ego that hates itself, the ego that says, 'You will never survive; if you go upon that stage and you sing, your voice will crack and everyone will laugh at you and throw tomatoes at you.' This is the ego which many others write about. So we must make sure to differentiate between my definition of ego which falls more in line with your definition of ego, and the ego that others communicate through spiritual teachings and writings of this day."

This is Jung speaking now. "For understand that as we bring these teachings through now...as we bring these teachings through now, we are bringing almost a combination of Freud and the current understanding of what an ego is. And what we want to bring to readers and we want to bring to people that are listening to these tapes or taking in these teachings is that they need to love their ego, they need to love the ego because the ego is unloved. They need to love it because the ego is their human. The ego is the human. And this is something that Michael and St. Germain did not say and I wanted to add to what they were saying. The best way to explain the ego is to say the human personality, period. The human personality without all the bells and whistles of all the multidimensionality. For the ego is the programmed human. That is the way that I see it. This may not be the correct way of seeing it, but this is the way that I see it, and this is my understanding and I wanted to share my perception because I think that it is important that we love all aspects of ourselves and most importantly we love those aspects of ourselves so that we are able to evolve into higher-dimensional aspects of ourselves. Therefore loving our soul, therefore loving the soul that we share with others, and therefore loving all humanity, because that piece of us inside of us that we think is so small that is the divine, that is the divine creator of all creation, is truly the biggest piece of us. But it is the piece that we are least likely to access while in physical form."

CHAPTER 15
THE FAT GUY

WILLIAM: With this truth, it seems to me that the most appropriate exercise would be an exercise in self love, because without self love we have nothing.

MARISA: St. Germain goes, "Oh, oh, we are going to do this, but, but, but we must, must, must introduce everyone to their ego, we must introduce them to their ego, for many will say, 'Oh, I call upon my higher self; I call upon St. Germain; I call upon Mother Mary,' but does anyone ever call their ego in? No. So, why don't we meet the ego?"

MARISA: Okay, Gayle I'm going to teach you how to ... we'll make a remote viewing address for the plane I'm going to ... 1163. Okay? So, that's my heart space that I go to. So 1163 is when I go into the "me" in the little balls here, and that's where I see all the guides coming in. When I channel the guides, like the earthbounds, I have to be in my bubble, so that's why it's harder for me, because I'm inside. But when I'm outside I'm gone. But look at that fat guy. Who is this fat guy that's following me now?

GAYLE: He's huge.

WILLIAM: He has nothing to do with anything.

MARISA: But he's standing where the... he's like a true imposter because he's standing where like the good guys stand.

GAYLE: Oh boy.

MARISA: Do you see him?

GAYLE: I can sense him. I can see him only because you've described him, but—

MARISA: He's fat and he has big pores on his arms and little hairs.

GAYLE: Yes. See, he doesn't feel like one thing. He feels like a compilation of gross—

MARISA: He's really gross.

GAYLE: Really gross. Just a compilation of gross.

WILLIAM: Well, what he is I can intuit, is ego gone wild. He is ego out of control satisfying every desire and every moment without any regard whatsoever for any other entities. You want to know about ego? I have a lot more questions on this one. This is a good one. This is going to be a big one...

MARISA: Are you sure because I don't understand?

WILLIAM: No, the lack of understanding is a plus because we don't want...I was even going to make a joke when we were talking about the egg. This isn't for eggheads. You had an example of eggs. I was going to say it's good you don't understand this because this isn't meant for eggheads. Because your need to understand in the simplest words is what's needed, because we don't want a book that's only for people that have got PhD's. That's not what we're writing for.

MARISA: No, exactly. Exactly. Yeah. They have to explain it to me, so I have to go in between and they don't have information that if we were, you know...I could go into trance...trance where I let them into my body when we did Source God, but then if we channel Source, and I go full, fully trance where I'm completely gone, then there's all the multi-dimensions and then they don't care about years and all that.

WILLIAM: That's okay.

MARISA: This guy over here is funny. I like him.

WILLIAM: Which one?

MARISA: The one with the stick. What's his name?

WILLIAM: Freud. Yeah, Freud. That's good because he wasn't particularly—

MARISA: He's going, "I demand—" He's got a really thick accent that one of my friends has. He reminds me of a concentration camp screaming Hitler guy or something. That's how angry he is. I mean it's funny how angry he is, because it's kind of cute because you can tell that he's not really angry; he's actually sad.

WILLIAM: Well, he is. I mean, first he had to leave Austria in 1938 because of the Nazis, and he died in exile in England. That's probably part of the reason why he died.

MARISA: What's 1918 then?

CHAPTER 16

1918 IS OUR GROUNDHOG YEAR

WILLIAM: 1918 – we're going to do an entire book, a skeptics guide to 1918.

MARISA: Oh.

WILLIAM: 1918 is the year—

MARISA: Is the beginning of all creation is what I just heard.

WILLIAM: Is the beginning of the alternative creation. Yeah. It's the beginning of this world which has a chance to survive. Had there not been implants in the human grid collective consciousness in 1918—well, in the universe in which that did not happen, human beings destroyed the planet. So, what we're here to do is to take the alternative branch, like a computer program, a game, and okay, we made some changes in 1918, we planted information in the grid. Let's see if that information is enough to prevent the destruction. And I can tell you right now, which is one of the good things—though not so good if you're attached to your human existence—it doesn't mean that this is going to work. There is still very much the real possibility that we are going to still destroy ourselves. But from the higher realms it doesn't' matter because they'll try it again. They'll go back to 1918 and put in more information. Or they'll go back to 1961 and put in more information and see if this time human beings make it.

MARISA: He said, "1918 is always where it starts."

WILLIAM: Okay. So 1918 will always be the year that it starts.

MARISA: I wonder what happened in that year.

WILLIAM: Well, one of the things, and this is interesting, we were going to bring this up. We might as well bring it up now. Around 1918, Charles Haanel released his book *The Master Key System.* We would like to know if that information, which included the first formulation of the law of attraction—

MARISA: Did they do something with steam? I just saw something with steam engines, I think. No, it's healing. But a transmutation of energy, where energy doesn't ever go away. Like water turns into steam, which turns into clouds, which turns into rain.

WILLIAM: Right. Well, that's part of the law of abundance. Charles Haanel's *The Master Key System* included the original formulations which are very popular today and were popularized in *The Secret* and other pop psychology books and films, the law of attraction, the law of abundance. And these laws, the universal mind, we're finding out through these skeptic's guidebooks and communications with the guides, are in fact universal laws that probably came to Charles Haanel through his higher self. So one of the questions I'd like to ask is did Charles Haanel quote "channel" *The Master Key System*, and if so, who were the guides that brought this information to the planet?

CHAPTER 17

CHARLES HAANEL WAS A CHANNEL

MARISA: "Who do you think brought it to the planet?"

WILLIAM: St. Germain.

MARISA: "Who do you think? I was the one that was put in charge in 1918. I was the one that was put in charge of the earth's evolution. I was the one that helped to create this matrix or this creation in which we are living. For it is something that we do in God school, in the third level of God school. We begin to work to recreate worlds that were hopeless, worlds that could not survive. For you will see, you will see when you get to this point, Bill, where you are able to take the consciousness which you are, into the God aspect, or into the ascended aspect of that which you are…you will begin to see and realize and know there are pieces of us that are always going and looking to see what did not succeed and trying to make it better. So I am part of this board as are 11 other ascended masters that are part of this board. Charles Haanel brought forth information from the...what this channel calls in her brain 'sixth plane of consciousness,' which is a combination between the fourth dimension, the sixth dimension, the eighth dimension, the tenth dimension and the twelfth dimension. For this is all the laws of the universe. This is the laws you speak of. All the laws of the universe. This is as they call it the Akashic records. This is the data of the universe. And it is interlaced within throughout the dimensions, and there are many people, Charles Haanel being one of them, that were able to tune into the databanks of the matrix that surrounds this universe and this galaxy where all of the rules reside. This channel being one that is able to tune into these layers and these are the healing information packets which we bring through during sessions and the information which Charles was able to bring through was information directly from Source facilitated by me. But you must understand that just as with any channel, he was only able to receive 40 percent of what we sent through, some of it being corrected by the mind, for he was intelligent indeed."

Was he smart?

WILLIAM: Very.

MARISA: Sixty percent intellectual mind, forty percent spirit...brought information through and the way that he built whatever you guys are talking about, I don't even know what it is, but whatever you guys are talking about—

WILLIAM: *The Master Key System.*

MARISA: Oh, is that the book that you wrote?

WILLIAM: We wrote the book *Tapping the Source*, which is the mini-version of *The Master Key System*. It was 100 years ago so we updated it and reduced 26 meditation techniques to seven focus phrases, and I am going to stress that in addition to whatever new exercise St. Germain may want to bless us with for how to capture the positive self love aspect of ego, that we include the seven focus phrases exercise because it's been proven effective as well.

MARISA: "Yes. We can do this indeed because these focus phrases that you speak of are for the ego, are for the, as many will call it, the little self, the human, the small self. Because what you must understand is that you as a human being are in essence at the center of your own universe being surrounded by all layers of self and the largest aspect of self being that which is God the Creator itself within you. You have all of these rules within you. You have all of this built up, all of these structures, all of these things that make someone into someone. So let us just go into the exercise."

CHAPTER 18
SELF LOVE EXERCISE

MARISA: "What we would like people to do is to just create a mirror within their mind. And what we would like for everyone who is reading this to do is to write down an issue. Write down an issue they have in their life, whether it is a good one, whether it is a bad one, whether it is a fear, whether it is something they are excited about. They are graduating. Let us just say 'We are graduating.' So we sit down and we say 'I am graduating.' What does my God self have to say about this?' And what you may do is you may close your eyes and you may take a few deep breaths in your nose and out your mouth, and just ask that a silver and gold and violet—of course we have to add violet—violet ball be sent down from a portal directly above the head.

"This ball of energy can be solid or it can be a bubble. It can be whatever one would like it to be. But ask that it get sent down directly from above and land around the individual. Continue to breathe in and out for about a minute and then one will be centered, one will be grounded, and one will be protected by anything outside of themselves. Now in your mind imagine a mirror. In this mirror you can see yourself. Is that mirror hazy? Can you see yourself clearly? Are you somebody else? What you must do now is ask that the God aspect of you show itself through all these layers of yourself in this mirror. Remember you're using your imagination. But you see this God aspect. This is the perfect piece of you, the perfect piece of you that you share with all others. Many will actually see a person. Many will see a light. Many will say, 'I am seeing nothing,' but that is because they are actually trying to see. You just must imagine. Whatever comes to your mind first. So you see that God aspect and you ask it how it feels about graduation. It may change the way it looks or it may stay the same. You can write down how it feels or you could just look to see.

"Now, after this, call in your soul. This is the piece of you inside of you. We will just call this a combination between the higher self and the spirit. This is your soul. It's your fifth-dimensional soul. So this is your soul. Call in your soul, tell it to step forward in this mirror, and show itself. Ask it how it feels about graduation. It may get brighter, it may say it is excited you have made it. It's congratulating you. It says it's proud of you. It says that you've done a good job. It's smiling.

"Now, ask your ego to step forward. What does your ego look like? Does your ego look like you? Does your ego look tired? Does your ego look awake? Ask your ego how it feels about graduation. Ask it to show you how it feels so you may feel what it feels like. You may start to feel anxiety. The first thing that comes to mind, you may say, 'Will I ever get a job? Now I have all these student loans. Oh my gosh, what am I going to do? What if my boyfriend or girlfriend breaks up with me right before graduation and then I look horrible at graduation? What if I trip walking across the stage? I should have graduated one year earlier. That other guy, he graduated a year earlier and I think he had a 4.0. I only had a 3.98. Oh my gosh I'm never going to make it. I'm never going to get a job.' And ask the ego, what do you need in order to feel better? What do you need in order to feel better? Everybody will get a different answer. But if it says love, maybe attention, maybe a pat on the head, or maybe it wants parents to tell everybody that you got a 3.98 and you're the best kid in the world. What does the ego want?

"Once you know what it wants, say it is love, say it is generosity, say it is peace. What we'd like for you to do is to imagine this as a big bucket above your head filled with a violet substance. As you pour this bucket down over your head as if, 'Wake up! Appreciate the world!'—you pour this over the ego in your imagination, and what happens is it dissolves. This is not dissolving your ego; it is dissolving the anger, it is dissolving the fear, it is dissolving the irrationality that it brings to you.

"So let us just say that we are not speaking of graduation. Let us just say that we are speaking of one day where homework needs to get done. Will the homework get done if the ego is not there saying that others are getting their homework done and you are not? Others are going to get an A on the test and you're not? Your parents are paying for this school and if you don't pass you're going to have to pay for it, and you're never going to get a job that's going to pay enough, so you better get your homework done so you can get good grades so that you can go out so you can get a job. You would never excel, you would never succeed, you would never make it in this world. You would just in essence be sitting on a cloud with a harp thinking that you're in heaven because there would be no duality, there would be no push, there would be no pull.

"But when the ego takes control of a situation that should be joyous, that should be happy, this is when we would like for you to become aware of it. When you begin to get emotional, when you begin to get angry, when you begin to get sad, depressed, stand in front of this mirror, ask your ego to step forward and ask it what it needs. If it needs compassion, imagine that compassion is the violet substance in this bucket and pour it over your head. They will dissolve in your imagination and this in essence is healing the ego. This will also bring an understanding to when the ego is taking control. When the ego is taking control you can never truly, truly be happy because even the greatest success will not be enough. But at the same time successes will not come without the ego. This is just human nature and there are going to be many that hate us for saying this, and many that truly oppose what we are saying, for they believe the ego is evil. But the ego is what makes us human. And the ego is our human. Ego is us in the physical plane. Does this make sense?"

WILLIAM: Of course.

MARISA: "So, we would like to also bring—if you would like for me to bring—an understanding of self love. We have done this in this exercise because what we are truly doing is we are asking the human piece of us what it needs from us, what it needs from us at any moment. And in doing this, what we are doing is we are actually nurturing ourselves by listening to ourselves. We are nurturing ourselves by bringing in understanding to what it is that we need at any given moment. Whereas most human beings, 98 percent of human beings on this planet, are completely unconscious of whether they are in ego, whether they are in their higher self, whether they are in their spirit, whether they are in their God consciousness. There are some that are able to get into their God consciousness. So, what one must begin to understand, to truly, truly evolve as a human being, a multidimensional human being that has access to all 12 dimensions and all the dimensions within those dimensions within those dimensions, the human being has access to all of them, we must understand where we're living from. Because just because we are sitting in one spot it does not mean that we cannot be living from 15 to 20 other spaces within ourselves and viewing life from that perspective...because truly life is all about perspective. And if you are perceiving life from the perspective of the ego, you are always going to feel left out, you are always going to feel defensive, you are always going to feel sad, you are always going to feel lack, you are always going to feel compared, you are always going to feel criticized. And that is just how life is. Does this make ego bad? No. It makes it necessary."

Chapter 19
Seven Focus Phrases

WILLIAM: Let's give one more short exercise that has been proven effective for thousands of people to connect with self love. It's based on the work of Charles Haanel. I actually am going to be reading from *The Complete Master Key System* published by Tarcher Penguin which is the revised, expanded version of the original book *Tapping the Source*. The authors of the book are myself William Gladstone—.

MARISA: St. Germain says, "And today if you buy one, you get two."

WILLIAM: —This is somewhat true. William Gladstone, Richard Greninger and John Selby. This isn't really a sales pitch though. If you want to go out and get a copy of this book, I think for those who resonate with it they will be greatly rewarded. And really the essence of the book you're about to get in this book, and it's very short, and as far as I've been able to determine, the most effective short method of entering into a meditative space that will immediately connect you at the deepest level with self love of the ego in a positive sense is:

One – I choose to focus enjoyably inward;

Two – My mind is quiet, I am now the silence;

Three – I am open to receive guidance from my source;

Four – I know what I want;

Five – I feel connected with creative power;

Six – My vision is right now perfect and complete;

Seven – Each new moment is manifesting my dream.

I want to call your attention to the fact that each of these focus phrases uses either the word "I" or "My." This is about connecting to the highest form of your ego in a positive way. This is really the basis of all meditation because you cannot connect with the source unless you exist, and you must exist at your highest possible level. And all of these phrases, from quieting your mind to focusing enjoyably inward, connects you with the core essence that is in fact you. So, on this level identifying with your ego is quite positive and in an almost ironic way by going within, you reach without because you're identifying yourself but then you're connecting with the source which is actually everything outside of you. So it's a way of creating a balance of that which is essentially you on the personality level with that which is essentially you on the cosmic level.

CHAPTER 20

ALPHEUS

MARISA: So Alpheus just wanted to come in and Alpheus is a godhead. He's in the fourth level of God school. We can talk about the different schools maybe in our next book. We are in soul school and we're shooting to become ascended, which means graduated from our soul university, and then we move onto God university and there are seven levels of God University. And he's in the fourth level. His name is Alpheus and he specializes in...this is what he's saying. I never knew he was in God school. This is cool. He's one of my guides. He specializes in sacred geometry, sound harmonics, and "meta-something" or other.

But he's showing me shapes and he's saying that "Actually everything you said is correct, but what we must explain is that when there is an intention and Charles Haanel had this intention to bring these frequencies or these statements into the center of one's being, that frequency will emit out into any aspect of self that is needed. So there was a piece of what was brought through to him that his intellectual mind was unable to hear. So if you can visualize within yourself a sphere, a spinning energy, this is within the solar plexus area, maybe a little higher, maybe a little lower, but this is where your consciousness is. Sometimes if you close your eyes and ask to see this sphere, it may be in a different spot. It may be up higher; it may be down lower. But what we would like for you to do is just imagine where this spinning sphere is—"

It looks like one of those fountains that has a ball in it and it kind of spins around. You know? Floats around.

"—inside of you. And when you say these statements imagine these statements going into the center of your consciousness. They will resonate out and find a pathway into the best possible place that they can go. Like a pebble running down a stream. It is going to go where it is easy. It is going to go where the channels are open. And these statements will open channels for information that will cause biofeedback within the cells of the thinking apparatus and the human body will show that these will raise the vibration.

"But if you just read them, yes, they are very effective. But if you read them and allow them to be read into the center of your consciousness, they will go to where they need to go. We have many shapes that you can imagine instead, or you can just read these and use the shape that I have given you."

It's opalescent, golden, silver. Opalescent like the abalone shell, how it has different colors when you shine on it. That's what it looks like. And it's silver. It's your God consciousness, basically. It's twelve. So he says, "Just ask where is that in my body?" Wherever it is, imagine it, and then read the statements and just read them and imagine that they're going into that and they will go where they need to go.

"Because what needs to be programmed—the ego does not necessarily need to be programmed, but the subconscious mind is truly, truly something that scientists, physicists and other researchers will discover soon that our subconscious mind is a roadmap to our entire multidimensionality. So by calling in these statements into this sphere of consciousness, you are actually reprogramming your subconscious mind over time."

Chapter 21
Fine Tuning Frequency

WILLIAM: I do want to acknowledge John Selby because I need to make it clear that these seven focus phrases are based on Charles Haanel's work, but were actually developed by my co-author and friend John Selby who studied at Princeton University, and for the past 40 years has been one of the premier proponents of stress reduction through meditation, and so it was a combination—

MARISA: So Charles Haanel actually worked with the frequencies, then, huh?

WILLIAM: Charles Haanel lived at the end of the 19th and early part of the 20th century. He got this information at the beginning of the 20th century.

MARISA: Not like electrical frequencies. Like healing frequencies. Is that what you mean?

WILLIAM: I don't have any documentation that he did, but he certainly, whether directly or indirectly, had an understanding because he was focused on teaching people the value of meditation to reach states that allow communication with what he called Universal Mind. Whether Charles Haanel initiated what is today known as the human development movement, he was the publicly acknowledged mentor of Napoleon Hill who wrote *Think and Grow Rich*. So most of the material that we have today about manifestation, the law of attraction, the law of abundance, really derives from the work of Charles Haanel. What John Selby added to this was an awareness of what works in a modern society where people at most have half an hour a day for meditation, and not the hours a day for meditation that Charles Haanel was requiring to master The Master Key System. So in the new book that is based on the *Tapping the Source* book that was re-released by Tarcher Penguin, we have John Selby's seven focus phrases. We do have the complete original *The Master Key System* in the back of the book for those who truly want to understand and have the time to go deeply within at the level of Charles Haanel. But for most people we have found that the seven focus phrases really are sufficient to raise their individual vibration and create a higher state of being, which does result in manifesting greater wealth, happiness and health.

MARISA: Yeah. And it must be Charles Haanel, what he's showing me is, they're showing him basically... they're bringing through all this information, all these frequencies. He was tuning into greater aspects of himself, of St. Germain. But there is just something in his mind that kept blocking stuff out. And the missing piece was actually bringing in the harmonious energies into the God center, as opposed to the human mind.

GAYLE: He was religious.

WILLIAM: That makes perfect sense. Yes, he had certain limitations on his—

MARISA: Oh   he   was   religious?   That   makes   sense because—

WILLIAM: Well, his father was a minister.

MARISA: Oh, okay. So he didn't believe that he was God? Or he didn't believe that he had God consciousness?

WILLIAM: No, he believed that he had found... he studied Hindu writings and other writings, and he believed that it was possible to communicate with what today we would call the zero point—which would be God consciousness or the Universal Mind—so he had very advanced beliefs for his day. But he lived and wrote about 100 years ago, so he did not have access to the information we have today. I think this exercise and the previous exercise are very helpful to people.

Chapter 22
Anthropology

WILLIAM: I want to finish this book by returning to some of the larger issues related to the world of psychology and what I would say are derivatives from William James' original work in terms of the field of anthropology. And so I would like to call upon, if he's available, the soul of Kroeber who was one of the founders of anthropology and ask him what he feels is the most important contribution he made to the field of anthropology and what in the field of anthropology is most useful to the average human being today.

MARISA: Did he find a bunch of fake stuff?

WILLIAM: I don't know. He probably did. There's been a lot of fake stuff for a long time.

MARISA: He just threw an axe pick thing in here. Anthropology is the—

WILLIAM: The study of man.

MARISA: That's like bones and stuff, right?

WILLIAM: No, that's archeology. Anthropology includes archeology.

MARISA: He just threw something through here.

WILLIAM: There's been many hoaxes and trying to—

MARISA: That's archeology. So anthropology is man. Humans.

WILLIAM: Yes.

MARISA: Because I'm seeing actual human bones.

WILLIAM: That's certainly part of anthropology. You have physical anthropology which includes archeology, then you have cultural anthropology which is what I studied at Harvard, and where Kroeber was much more important. One of his students was Margaret Mead who is of course very well known as having studied sexual practices.

MARISA: She's kind of snooty.

WILLIAM: In Samoa and elsewhere she was revered by many, many people. One of her legacy statements was "Is it really possible that a small group of individuals can change the world?" And her response: "Why, it's the only thing that ever has." So, she was quite inspiring in the field. But back to Kroeber. Alfred Kroeber is known as the father of

American anthropology, cultural anthropology. Though he did study archeology. He received the very first doctorate awarded in anthropology by Columbia University. That was in 1901. I'm most interested in Kroeber as the creator of the concept of the super organic. And the concept of the super organic is very intriguing. It actually has not been a concept that modern anthropologists spend much time studying. The reason I'm interested in it, it seems to relate very much to the worldview being presented in these books that we are all connected at a higher level. The super organic was Kroeber's way of formulating the connection that existed at a level of the super unconscious, the collective unconscious I should say, which unites all of the intelligence of the earth. His concepts were quite controversial and still not accepted by most of mainstream anthropology. So, I'd like to know if Kroeber's soul—

MARISA: So what's his name?

WILLIAM: Alfred Kroeber.

MARISA: Alfred Kroeber. Okay, so a big huge guy just came in. He's coming from Pleiades. That's where his soul is coming from.

WILLIAM: Right.

MARISA: He's not alive. When you said, I don't remember what word you just said, but you said something and I saw the egg thing again and I saw these little sunshine rays around it, and then down here there is a circle, looks like donuts, but they're connected. That's what they're showing me. All these little donut things. And then as soon as one of these donuts gets near this one with the sunshine things around it, it gets all these sunshines around it. I don't know what that means. It looks like cells or something affecting each other.

WILLIAM: Well, part of it was his concept that the collective unconscious exists, and it's probably primary to the concept of the noosphere from Teilhard de Chardin that maintains that all of intelligence on planet earth—

MARISA: It's all connected.

WILLIAM: —is all connected and—

MARISA: Okay, so this is what he says. He goes, "Argh, argh..." He's so loud. So he says, "Yes, yes, I come in full form, yes, yes, yes. Okay, fine."

Was he short?

WILLIAM: Probably. You know, he was from a previous... he had a beard.

MARISA: He's projecting like he's... yeah, he's projecting like he's huge and he kind of reminds me of Abraham Lincoln with the—I don't know if he has a hat on or what—but he's projecting himself like he's humongous and a lot of times people that weren't so tall in this life will project themselves as humongous beings. So, he looks really big.

He's pretty clear, actually. Hopefully we'll be able to talk to him. He's good at speaking in pictures. Let me just explain for the book what he's explaining to me ... it's again these little eggs. He's showing me, he's calling it a nucleus. There's a circle and then it has another circle around it, and then on the outside it looks like little jagged, sunshine rays almost, you know like when little kids draw the sunshine. And there's a bunch of little triangles on the outside of the sphere. And then it shows a shot, almost like a rope, a string shooting from there and there's another one with the energy around it, energy around a cell. But then on the bottom over here on the left I see a bunch of them without those little rays around them. And he's showing that the one up top, if it touches another one it affects it, and then that one affects that, and then all of them have the stuff around them. And he's saying, "Nothing happens without something happening before it. Everything happens because of a—"

I don't know if it's a nucleus or a cell. I don't have the words for it, but he's showing this interconnectedness, like cause and effect type understanding of not only human consciousness but the cells that we're made up of. Did he study human cells in a petri dish or something?

WILLIAM: No.

MARISA: Then what are these things that he's showing me? I think it's consciousness, I think they're souls.

WILLIAM: Yes. He was an abstract thinker. I mean he was a very prolific anthropologist. He wrote six major works and he studied everything. So, he touched on everything. But what I'm particularly interested in, he was the first anthropologist to truly discuss the way culture shapes human behavior and how culture evolves from humans but actually exists beyond humans.

MARISA: Well, that's what he's saying. He's saying, "The energy of one affects another and that one is not one without being affected by another."

So what you're talking about is culture. So, what he is saying is that this outside thing out here affects, hold on ... stop drawing me pictures. I want him to channel. He can't get it to me, though. What I've found is they cannot get into my field if they're not part of my soul group. That's what I've realized. I can channel them, I can say what they're saying, but they can't ... like how Einstein or these guys over here can get in.

WILLIAM: Well, ask him if he's part of my soul group.

MARISA: No. He's not. He's on Pleiades. But we can still channel him. He just can't step into my energy. That's why he was going "argh, argh ..." He was yelling to me outside of the energy. Okay, hold on, let's see. "All of humanity is affected by the energy that is around it at any particular time."

What was your specific question for him? What his idea about—

CHAPTER 23

THE COLLECTIVE UNCONSCIOUSNESS AND THE SUPER ORGANIC

WILLIAM: The collective unconscious and the super organic. Those are the two concepts that most intrigue me.

MARISA: The super organic is God, right?

WILLIAM: Well, ask him.

MARISA: That's what he said. Or...yeah, he's saying its God, it's the underlying energy within all. He says: "So when I say that everything is affected by something, what I mean is that there is one that is stationary, there is one that is always one, there is one that is un-affectable, but then when one creates another it becomes affectable and is in relation to the un-affectable aspect of that which is affectible by that which it is surrounded by."

Oh, that's what he's talking about. The unaffected. The affected is the bigger circle and then it touches the other, it affects that.

WILLIAM: And let me restate this in simpler language. He's really talking about cultural practices. Human beings develop cultural practices, and every culture has its own cultural practices, its own mores, its own traditions. Those traditions persist after the individual human beings who created them cease to exist, and impact the individuals who were born into those cultures. So, it's in that level that I always interpreted the super organic because it's beyond organic. What is a culture? A culture has no energetic parts other than consciousness. It has no physical parts. A custom is not made up of molecules unless we discover that consciousness has molecules. So that to me is the formulation of the super organic. Interestingly, okay, we have the super organic as a concept; now we have the even more outrageous concept of the collective unconscious. Remember, this is a concept from the early part of the 20th century. The idea of collective unconscious was absolutely outrageous in that somehow all ideas are part of a collective unconscious, a collective unconscious that continues to exist after the individuals who had this consciousness created it. And it persists into future and future generations. So my question is, where did Kroeber get the concept of the collective unconscious, and what value does he see this concept having related to the information that we've been receiving from St. Germain and the other guides as to the connective nature of reality on the higher dimensions?

MARISA: "Let us just start with this, let us just start with this, that the collective unconsciousness can change at any given time. The collective unconsciousness is forever shifting, forever changing, and affected by consciousness, whether it be consciousness within the physical or consciousness within the ethers. For, consciousness is forever changing as is the collective unconscious. For, the—"

What is that? Super organic? Is that what you called it?

WILLIAM: Yes.

MARISA: "The super organic is what we would call the unchangeable unconscious. For that is the stationary and the solid consciousness of that which is, and is affected by matter and matter is affected by it. For, as I stand back and as I look at this petri dish of a planet, it is fascinating to me to see and realize where the information that I was getting while on the earth plane was coming from. For, it was coming from a field that surrounds this planet, a field that surrounds any planet. There is a field that carries the thoughts, the consciousness, the awareness, the beliefs, the diagrams of all of humanity and that which is and that which will be based on the principles of the laws of the universe, in that if I choose as God consciousness, unchanging God consciousness, to offer and exist within the consciousness of a human being, I will then and thereby be affected by, as you say, the cultures.

"But it is not just the cultures. It is the fields of consciousness that one is connected to. This is what I am showing in this diagram which this channel is seeing, is that there are fields with information, fields with rules, fields with different dynamics, different cultures, different nationalities, different layers of government, different layers of social standing. And all these different labels, all of these different types of beings, different types of things, places, aspects of this planet, are all fields that the unconscious, the conscious are plugged into and affected by on the earth plane.

"This is me standing back, staring up at that which is the earth plane, looking upon this as this, as you have been calling a virtual reality, and seeing how human beings are affected by this. Yes, cultures far surpass and continue to survive past having human beings that will respect, honor, and live within them because they are fields. They are beings of their own, if you would like to look at them as their own being. So, if a culture or if an aspect of the earth plane is its own being in essence in the dimension in which it exists, then we can always be affected by it, we can always for the lack of a better word, tune into it and take into us or our consciousness the aspects of it.

"For, abstract thinking, yes, you say to me abstract thinking is the way that I thought within the earth plane. I saw in pictures, I dreamt in pictures, I spoke in pictures. For this is what I saw and I had to bring about an understanding into the mind what it—"

He's basically going "what the heck it meant." He's showing all these weird honeycomb pictures and shapes and he says "tetrahedrons" and "pentagons" and "spheres" and "pyramids." Was he a mathematician of any sort?

WILLIAM: Not by training, no.

MARISA: Not a mathematician. Not geometry. It looks like geometry, you know, but it's not geometry. Oh! Sacred geometry. It's sacred geometry. But what was his whole basis of his teachings? I still don't understand. Well, I didn't hear a thing he said, actually but—

WILLIAM: He was an anthropologist. He started—

MARISA: He studied man, right?

WILLIAM: He studied human behavior. He started, you know, with studying cultural artifacts, archeology.

MARISA: That's the bone he threw at me.

WILLIAM: Probably the bones. He studied all that. He's best known actually for his study of indigenous Americans.

CHAPTER 24
KROEBER'S LEGACY

MARISA: That's the ape he had in his hands in the beginning. And then when you said, "No, not archeology," because I saw the bone pick, and then I said, "Ah then you're a hitchhiker." But now you said that, he goes, "No, no, no. Look..." So, let me follow this stream. So, he threw the pick, he found a bone, there's an ape over there and the ape is kind of looking at him. They're giving me a cartoon, a visual. But it's fake. And he got all excited but it was fake. And he got frustrated. And it looks like he decided that he was going to study stuff that was less tangible, almost, and so that's when he got into really sitting for hours upon hours, but it would be in nature, out where you would see someone digging. But he would just be out there. And he would see these shapes coming in, and it's the shapes that I'm drawing that he would see. And then all of a sudden he would have these theories and he would just write them down, and that's kind of what came to him. And some stuff came to him in dreams, he said. And it all came from his higher self.

WILLIAM: So, my question for his higher self is what does he feel his legacy is as the father of American anthropology, and what is his view of 2016 anthropological work?

MARISA: He's basically saying...he just stepped back. Okay, come forward. Can you just give me the definition of anthropology for my brain to know?

WILLIAM: It's the study of man, human behavior.

MARISA: That's what I thought. Yeah.

WILLIAM: It's the study of human behavior and culture.

MARISA: Because what he's saying is that he feels—I don't know if that's now or then—but he's saying that he feels that he brought a greater understanding to what man was. Instead of a monkey with a bone, it was a greater understanding that we're more than just the flesh and bones, and that there's layers to us, and those layers help bring an understanding to who we are; not just the bones. And that we far outlive the bones and the flesh by the consciousness and the thought that we leave behind. And he's showing those as the shapes.

WILLIAM: Well, in modern language he's referred to as the father of cultural anthropology, specifically, and it certainly is true that culture is far more than the artifacts that a culture creates. And on that level one could associate a culture as a consciousness. So, that was what his pioneering work was about.

MARISA: But he's saying that, yeah, it's way more than just...hold on. Good, he came back in. He stepped out and then he stepped back in. Okay, he says, "Scientists today, the ones who have incarnated on this planet as scientists, do bring in abstract thinking, do bring in a greater under-standing, and do bring in what you would call channeled works, but we just bring in a higher understanding. We would like to say that many times you are not channeling, you are just bringing in a higher understanding because it is a higher aspect of your brain. Because it is your brain that is still channeling this information. It is still your brain; it is still your human.

This is St. Germain speaking now. "So, this will lend to Bill's idea that the human mind is the genius because it in fact is, because it is the radio that is picking up on the frequency that is coming in, when in all reality the frequency that is coming in is coming from within, because it is coming from the higher self that is inside of us."

WILLIAM: Thank you St. Germain for the acknowledg-ment, and again thank you Dr. Kroeber—

MARISA: But he says it's not the ego, and you—

WILLIAM: No, no. But thank you for acknowledging the importance of the vehicle, because the genius comes from without but could not be received unless the vehicle is attuned and kept in good working order.

MARISA: Well, technically the higher self is within, so it is inside; it's just what the brain is picking up on. So this guy, I forgot his name already, the one with the bone and the pick axe.

WILLIAM: Kroeber.

MARISA: He just said that he feels if he wouldn't have come along, and he wouldn't have brought along a better understanding to legacies or what's in the fields around, that he believes people wouldn't have an understanding of how you can move to a place and start to act different, and it's because of the fields that that place is tuned into.

WILLIAM: So, another question for Kroeber—we've learned that 1918 was a pivotal year. What occurred in the life of Dr. Kroeber in 1918 in terms of him becoming a staple for imprinting this new level of awareness on planet Earth?

CHAPTER 25
THE BIG SECRET

MARISA: Ooh, it's a big secret. He just went, "What are you talking about?" St. Germain went, "Shh."

WILLIAM: Come on guys.

MARISA: St. Germain goes, "Don't tell them it's not real. Shh, the other soul groups don't know." He's going "Shh" and the guides are looking at me like "Huh?"

WILLIAM: Don't play dumb here. Come on Kroeber, fess up. St. Germain, come on, do your stuff.

MARISA: Kroeber doesn't know anything about this alternate reality, that's for sure. Was he even alive at that time?

WILLIAM: Yes, he was alive in 1918.

MARISA: In the '40's though?

WILLIAM: I believe he passed in 1950. What year in the '50s?

GAYLE: It says 1960.

WILLIAM: Oh he lived until 1960.

GAYLE: He was 84.

WILLIAM: Yeah. He had a good, long life.

MARISA: He says the '40's were the prime of his existence.

WILLIAM: Career, yeah. Okay so he wasn't... he may have brought something in without even knowing it.

MARISA: Yeah, he says '42 was the prime of his existence. Because he says "1918? 1942 was the prime of my existence." And then St. Germain goes, "Shh, don't tell them it's an alternate reality." St. Germain says some of the soul groups that are operating and existing in this realm are operating and existing in it based on the fact that they're not going to know that they're the soul groups that destroyed the planet.

WILLIAM: Okay, but one of the good points that has come from this is it is clear that individual souls and human beings may have played pivotal roles without awareness of their roles.

MARISA: St. Germain says: "Oh absolutely, absolutely. Ninety percent of the planet does not know this. You must know this, for this is a creation upon a creation. But look at it this way: your soul in another reality could be existing in someone else's reality at this very moment without you even knowing."

WILLIAM: Well, thank you very much, Kroeber. I want to end this book by returning to our two main men for the study of psychology, and I do apologize that we haven't really honored the female heritage of the study of psychology. There are many great female psychologists.

MARISA: Is there a Marilyn? Did you already say Marilyn Dowell or something?

WILLIAM: Well, I talked about Margaret Mead.

MARISA: No, not Margaret Mead. Something like Marilyn Dowell. I keep hearing someone screaming that name and I don't know—

WILLIAM: I'm not aware of that. I'm not a student of—

GAYLE: There is a Marilyn Dowell.

MARISA: There is?

GAYLE: Yes.

MARISA: Who is she? Look her up. I'm hearing it screamed.

WILLIAM: Yeah, I will confess I'm not a student of psychology. I was a student of anthropology at Harvard. And I'm only aware of—.

MARISA: So, anthropology, one thing they're saying is, they mostly all believed that we evolve from apes, right?

WILLIAM: Yes.

MARISA: Okay, so that's why he was throwing the pick axe, because he was saying that when he died he realized that we didn't evolve from apes, and he said it was one of those a-ha moments. And he said it was probably the most glorious moment in his existence as this personality because it then explained so much. Because there was always this missing link or gap between how one could have happened to another and how one was unaffected, because he believed that everything was affected by something else, and that there was something missing or something, but—

WILLIAM: Well, if we didn't evolve from apes, what species did we evolve from?

MARISA: "Humans."

WILLIAM: Well, but humans didn't appear without being part of the great chain of being, or is it there is no great chain of being?

MARISA: "Well..."

WILLIAM: I mean, we know if we go all the way back we started as a rock, and then we evolved and we evolved.

MARISA: "Rocks are created beings, apes are created beings, humans are created beings. Everything is a created being by a Creator Being but there are other worlds, other places, other realities, other dimensions where humans have been tinkered with, humans have been played with. So the humans that existed on the earth plane to begin with were very ape-like, were very animalistic, and this is when God consciousness said, 'Oh, they are evolved enough, I will go live in them.' And as this God consciousness with these soul bodies, with these light bodies choose to incarnate into these ape-like humans, this is when the physical form begins to take shape around the light body form. Because in all actuality, the spiritual body creates the physical body."

WILLIAM: And the first humanoids, is what they're called, appeared. I know you don't like dates but how many thousands of years ago?

MARISA: I'm not going to ask him. I'm just going to ask up there. They're actually showing not billions, not millions. They are taking me back to 42,000 years ago.

WILLIAM: That is the last extinction.

MARISA: But they're showing me 8,000 years or something like that, but then they're going back to 11,000 and they're showing me a little representation of Adam and Eve being these evolved humans; but then they're showing these ape-like people outside of their garden.

WILLIAM: The Neanderthals.

MARISA: Yeah, that's the word. Neanderthal.

WILLIAM: We had the Neanderthals and Cro-Magnon man.

MARISA: And there were giants. They're showing me there were giants. And there were little tiny people too. There were small people and giants.

WILLIAM: The Menehune of Hawaii.

MARISA: But there were humans that were like ape-like enough that bred with apes.

WILLIAM: Okay. I believe that this will have to be covered in another book, "A Skeptic's Guide To Evolution." But we'll save that for the moment. I don't know who this Marilyn Dowell is. If she's...was she a psychologist?

GAYLE: She passed in 2015. She was religious. And about community.

WILLIAM: So she really doesn't have any connection to this discussion.

GAYLE: She may just be somebody who—

WILLIAM: She's just trying to get a free ride here.

MARISA: Yeah. I wonder why she...that was so random.

GAYLE: She just popped in.

WILLIAM: In any event, so I was apologizing that there's not many women represented here other than Margaret Mead. I really was not exposed in school to any pioneering psychologists or anthropologists because there weren't that many females in any of those fields. I mean, it's only recently that women were even permitted to go to college.

Chapter 26
Freud and Jung

WILLIAM: So, let's just go back to the two people that I feel made the greatest contributions to modern psychology—mainly Freud and Jung. And I just want to end with, more curiosity—I think we've received deep insights already—but I'm not sure if either or both would like to speak a little bit about the feud between them because they were good friends and then they were no longer good friends. And if they could explicate a little bit for those who are interested in their lives, what caused the rift, and if after passing into the higher dimensions they've been able to become good friends again?

MARISA: "Oh yes, we are friends, we always were friends and we always will be friends. When the human mind begins to go, one gets grumpy, cranky, and really very hard to be around."

That Carl Jung, did he start to go insane at the end of his life?

WILLIAM: Well, I don't know.

MARISA: He looks like…they both look like they were going crazy towards the end of their lives.

WILLIAM: It's very possible.

MARISA: Yeah. It looks like they're both starting to go crazy. They said that they've always been friends. They were never not friends. There was some form of a feud in the way of one believed in multidimensionality; one did not. One just believed that it was all about the vehicle, the body, the mind. The other believed that there was something else to it. And it was just kind of like a conflict in the belief system. And that Jung thought that Freud's was too elementary, and based too much on outside sources like people affecting you when you were little, and that he felt that it was much greater than that. And we have much more control over who we were and what we were. That we were not just these robots programmed by stuff before we even could know who we were. And he's showing that…they never really had a real feud-feud, they were definitely—

WILLIAM: It was hyped up in the press—

MARISA: Yeah. They definitely remained friends and they always were friends. They were dear friends. And it shows that they've been brothers in several lifetimes. They were in Atlantis together. They were here together. And they're literally standing right next to each other.

WILLIAM: Well, Jung was more adventuresome in terms of exploring ideas like archetypes and animus, which is the concept of the soul. Freud as you've just said really focused on the vehicle. And Jung much more on the connections to what we would now call the higher self. I would just like each of them to make a parting comment as to what they hope their legacy is able to generate at this specific time, 2016, on our planet. And I want to thank both of them for not only everything that they contributed while in human form, but also for everything they are continuing to contribute from the other side.

MARISA: Jung says, "Thank you." Jung says, "If a greater understanding could come to and larger credit could come to the greater pieces of us or the fields that surround us without diminishing the importance of the human in which we exist, this would be something that would please me indeed. This would be something that would complete me, and help me to feel whole in the work that I brought to the planet while there. For, when I was there I did not have a true complete understanding of the, as you call, higher self, but I had an understanding that there was something greater-than. You would maybe call it a... not a higher self, but something that was higher than the self. The way that I understood, I did not know whether I understood it as God or the higher self or a soul. I just knew that there was something that was in essence not of that being that could affect the being, but that it was controllable. For, understand that as human beings evolve down the path of evolution, as human beings begin to understand our multidimensionality, they will come to a better understanding of what I saw, what I explained, and what I taught. For, many times great researchers, great professors, great scientists are ahead of their time. Great scientists will come in with information, place it into the grid through being incarnated, place it into the earth just by being incarnated, write about it. But no one will understand it, and then years and years will pass by and it will begin to be understood. For, the understanding of the work that I did and—"

Did he write anything in 1932?

WILLIAM: I'm sure he did.

MARISA: "1932...the works of 1932 will be brought to the forefront of human understanding as the extra cavities within the brain are beginning to be understood. For, there are parts of the brain that human researchers have not even begun to understand in any way, shape or form. They believe they understand it but as they begin to understand this more they will realize that more and more consciousness can be allowed within the physical body. I did not understand this while I was alive, but I sensed it. There was a deep-seated feeling inside of me that I could understand these concepts, but I truly did not understand. And that is the reason why I stay within these fields, within these planes, so that I can watch and see the fruits of my labor, and I can help other students of the mind, other students of humans, other students of philosophy, even students of religion and spirituality, because I encompass all of these fields."

Freud says, "Alright, alright, alright." Whack with his stick. "Let me talk, let me talk, let me talk." And he goes, "Ma, shut up!" He started screaming at her. He says: "Ugh. Okay. So if we keep taking the focus off the human we will forget that we are human, and that is the whole reason for being here. That's all I have to say. Thank you, goodbye." He just turned around on his heel and walked away.

WILLIAM: Well, actually I want to follow up on what Freud just said because I think it actually is extremely important and it is part of my ongoing dialogue with St. Germain. I think that we need to respect and honor human beings as human beings, for all they have done, most of them without any awareness over the last hundred, two hundred years, that they even had a higher self. And it is really building upon the work of people like Kroeber, like Spinoza, like Freud, Jung, that we achieve a better understanding at the human level that we can communicate as human beings that may create the higher awareness that is necessary for the salvation of the species of the planet. And even if we're nothing more than the equivalent of a virtual reality game from a higher dimension, I think it's quite admirable that we're playing our roles—at least some of us are playing our roles—with true passion and human frailty and achieving greater awareness. And yes, ultimately, all of that greater awareness is coming from our higher selves and the higher planes, but without the commitment as human beings, at a human level, not only would we not have achieved what we've achieved to date, but there wouldn't be—and I say this from the part of myself that comes from the future—there will be no practical future unless we continue to identify in our ego with the best of each of us in terms of our personality as we move forward and progress beyond the limitations of our human ego. So, I want to thank very much all of the contributors to this incredible conversation book, and we look forward to the future books which may touch on the topics of "A Skeptic's Guide To Evolution" and "A Skeptic's Guide To 1918" and some of the other quite interesting concepts that have been presented here and in previous books.

MARISA: They want to give one more exercise. One more exercise.

WILLIAM: Okay.

CHAPTER 27
A FINAL EXERCISE

MARISA: And it's not St. Germain. It's actually Alpheus, it looks like. He says, "For each reader today, what we would like to bring to you is a brain activation, a mind activation in bringing your higher self, in bringing your God consciousness, in bringing all of the quote/unquote 'upper aspects of you' into the brain, so that you are able to unleash the genius within. So you are able to open up the cavities that have been calcified. So that you are able to open up the areas and the pathways that have not been used for years and years and years and years, sometimes maybe not ever been used. So, what we would like for you to do is to imagine that you have a brain. This is your brain. This is it in a jar. Or you can imagine it in your head—however is easier to imagine this.

"Imagine a brain with all of the divots, with all of the canals, all of the indents on the brain. Now imagine a beautiful silver liquid pouring down over this and filling your head, filling up your skull completely with this silver energy. What you are doing is filling your head with your higher consciousness, with the energy of your higher consciousness. You are replacing any negative frequencies, any negative energy, any blocks, any beliefs 'I am stupid, I am dumb, I don't understand; I am just 15 years old, I am only 20; I am 50, I have lost my intelligence'—whatever it is that you have within your mind that keeps you from a greater understanding of who you are, what you are, where you are going, with a thirst for a knowledge, with a desire to be a human, with a desire to allow yourself to be human with a higher self that lives within the human; not a higher self that is outside of the human.

"So we are bringing heaven to earth. We are bringing the higher self into the human. We are merging spirit with matter by allowing you to bring the frequency of your creator self into the human brain. Just imagine that this liquid is coming into your head or imagine your brain in a jar or some sort of visualization where you can see that the silver is completely surrounding your brain. And what you are doing is you are asking your higher self to saturate your human mind, your intellectual mind, your ego, your subconscious mind, your pineal gland—all the glands within the brain—with the creator energy. And you will become more creative, you will become smarter. You will remember things that you have not remembered for a very long time, maybe not ever. You will remember past lives maybe, you will remember what your path is. You will begin to remember because when human beings are bathing themselves in spirituality, they leave ... they leave their human body.

"They go into their higher self and they roam about the astral planes. They go into the ethers, they go up into other worlds, other places that are non-local, non-local realities; but they do not stay within the mind, within the body. And our bodies are truly, truly their own universe, truly their own reality. And if you can call your God consciousness in to saturate the mind each day, you will see changes, your vibration will go up, you will become smarter, you will become more intelligent, and you will be more in alignment with the genius that you are, the genius that you have been and the genius that you always will be—a creator God incarnate. We bless each one of you and we bid you adieu."

And St. Germain says: "Adieu, adieu, adieu."

WILLIAM: And adieu to you, too.

Made in the USA
Monee, IL
07 July 2026

56552031R00069